Silly snacks

Publications International, Ltd.
Favorite Brand Name Recipes at www.fbnr.com

Pictured on the front cover: Lady Bugs *(page 108)*.

Pictured on the back cover *(left to right):* Little Piggy Pie *(page 35)* and Silly Snake Sandwich *(page 58)*.

Microwave Cooking: Microwave ovens vary in wattage. Use the cooking times as guidelines and check for doneness before adding more time.

Preparation/Cooking Times: Preparation times are based on the approximate amount of time required to assemble the recipe before cooking, baking, chilling or serving. These times include preparation steps such as measuring, chopping and mixing. The fact that some preparations and cooking can be done simultaneously is taken into account. Preparation of optional ingredients and serving suggestions is not included.

Table of Contents

Snack Attack!

You never know when your child's need to snack is going to attack. Now you can be ready! These super-simple, sweet and savory snacks are sure to hit the spot.

Super Spread Sandwich Stars

1 Red or Golden Delicious apple, peeled, cored and coarsely chopped
1 cup roasted peanuts
⅓ cup honey
1 tablespoon lemon juice
1 teaspoon ground cinnamon
Sliced sandwich bread

For Super Spread, place chopped apple, peanuts, honey, lemon juice and cinnamon in food processor or blender. Pulse food processor several times until ingredients start to blend, occasionally scraping down the sides with rubber spatula. Process 1 to 2 minutes until mixture is smooth and spreadable.

For Sandwich Stars, use butter knife to spread about 1 tablespoon Super Spread on 2 slices of bread. Stack them together, spread side up. Top with third slice bread. Place cookie cutter on top of sandwich; press down firmly and evenly. Leaving cookie cutter in place, remove excess trimmings with your fingers or a butter knife. Remove cookie cutter.

Makes 1¼ cups spread (enough for about 10 sandwiches)

Favorite recipe from **Texas Peanut Producers Board**

Dizzy Dogs

1 package (8 breadsticks) refrigerated breadstick dough
1 package (16 ounces) hot dogs (8 hot dogs)
1 egg white
  Sesame seeds and poppy seeds
  Mustard, ketchup and barbecue sauce (optional)

1. Preheat oven to 375°F.

2. Using 1 piece breadstick dough for each, wrap hot dogs with dough in spiral pattern. Brush breadstick dough with egg white and sprinkle with sesame and poppy seeds. Place on ungreased baking sheet.

3. Bake 12 to 15 minutes or until light golden brown. Serve with condiments for dipping, if desired.   *Makes 8 hot dogs*

Banana Tot Pops

3 firm, medium DOLE® Bananas
6 large wooden sticks
½ cup raspberry or other flavored yogurt
1 jar (1¾ ounces) chocolate or rainbow sprinkles

• Cut each banana crosswise in half. Insert wooden stick into each half.

• Pour yogurt into small bowl. Hold banana pop over bowl; spoon yogurt to cover all sides of banana. Allow excess yogurt to drip into bowl. Sprinkle candies over yogurt.

• Place pops on wax paper-lined tray. Freeze 2 hours.

Makes 6 servings

Prep Time: 20 minutes
Freeze Time: 2 hours

Dizzy Dogs

Take-Along Snack Mix

1 tablespoon butter or margarine
2 tablespoons honey
1 cup toasted oat cereal, any flavor
½ cup coarsely broken pecans
½ cup thin pretzel sticks, broken in half
½ cup raisins
1 cup "M&M's"® Chocolate Mini Baking Bits

In large heavy skillet over low heat, melt butter. Add honey; stir until blended. Add cereal, nuts, pretzels and raisins; stir until all pieces are evenly coated. Continue cooking over low heat 10 minutes, stirring frequently. Remove from heat; immediately spread on waxed paper until cool. Add "M&M's"® Chocolate Mini Baking Bits. Store in tightly covered container.   *Makes about 3½ cups*

Bagelroonies

6 onion bagels
6 tablespoons soft-spread margarine
1 (14-ounce) jar NEWMAN'S OWN® Sockarooni™ Sauce
1 (8-ounce) package Canadian bacon slices
1 (16-ounce) package mozzarella cheese, shredded (2 cups)
Freshly grated Parmesan cheese

Cut bagels in half; spread with margarine. Spoon Newman's Own® Sockarooni sauce onto bagel halves, approximately 3 tablespoons per bagel half. Chop Canadian bacon slices and place over sauce. Sprinkle liberally with shredded mozzarella cheese. If desired, shake grated Parmesan cheese over bagels. Broil until cheese melts and bubbles.   *Makes 6 servings*

Note: If desired, sprinkle with mushrooms, olives, or jalapeños.

Take-Along Snack Mix

Peanut Butter and Jelly Pizza Sandwich

1 English muffin
2 tablespoons JIF® Creamy Peanut Butter
2 tablespoons SMUCKER'S® Strawberry Jam
6 to 8 slices banana
Chocolate syrup
Sweetened, flaked coconut (optional)

1. Split and toast English muffin. Spread JIF® peanut butter on both sides of the English muffin. Spread SMUCKER'S® Strawberry Jam on JIF® peanut butter.

2. Top with banana slices. Drizzle on chocolate syrup to taste. Sprinkle with coconut flakes, if desired. Eat while still warm.   *Makes 1 serving*

Pizza Rollers

1 package (10 ounces) refrigerated pizza dough
½ cup pizza sauce
18 slices turkey pepperoni
6 sticks mozzarella cheese

1. Preheat oven to 425°F. Coat baking sheet with nonstick cooking spray.

2. Roll out pizza dough on baking sheet to form 12×9-inch rectangle. Cut pizza dough into 6 (4½×4-inch) rectangles. Spread about 1 tablespoon sauce over center third of each rectangle. Top with 3 slices pepperoni and stick of mozzarella cheese. Bring ends of dough together over cheese, pinching to seal. Place seam side down on prepared baking sheet. Bake in center of oven 10 minutes or until golden brown.   *Makes 6 servings*

Peanut Butter and Jelly Pizza Sandwich

Wafflewich

2 frozen cinnamon waffles
25 miniature marshmallows
2 tablespoons JIF® Creamy Peanut Butter
½ banana, sliced
¼ cup chocolate chips

1. Toast waffles in toaster until desired darkness.

2. Heat miniature marshmallows and JIF® in microwave until melted, then mix together.

3. Spread JIF® peanut butter mixture on waffle.

4. Place banana slices on JIF® peanut butter mixture.

5. Top with chocolate chips.

6. Close sandwich with other waffle.   *Makes 1 wafflewich*

Wafflewiches taste best when eaten while they are still warm!

Wafflewich

Kids' Quesadillas

8 slices American cheese
8 (10-inch) flour tortillas
½ pound thinly sliced deli turkey
6 tablespoons *French's®* **Sweet & Tangy Honey Mustard**
2 tablespoons melted butter
¼ teaspoon paprika

1. To prepare 1 quesadilla, arrange 2 slices of cheese on 1 tortilla. Top with ¼ of the turkey. Spread with *1½ tablespoons* mustard, then top with another tortilla. Prepare 3 more quesadillas with remaining ingredients.

2. Combine butter and paprika. Brush one side of tortilla with butter mixture. Preheat 12-inch nonstick skillet over medium-high heat. Arrange tortilla butter side down and cook 2 minutes. Brush top of tortilla with butter mixture and turn over. Cook 1½ minutes or until golden brown. Repeat with remaining 3 quesadillas.

3. Slice into wedges before serving.   *Makes 4 servings*

Prep Time: 5 minutes
Cook Time: 15 minutes

Kids' Quesadillas

Grilled Cheese & Turkey Shapes

8 teaspoons *French's®* **Mustard, any flavor**
8 slices seedless rye or sourdough bread
8 slices deli roast turkey
4 slices American cheese
2 tablespoons butter or margarine, softened

1. Spread *1 teaspoon* mustard on each slice of bread. Arrange turkey and cheese on half of the bread slices, dividing evenly. Cover with remaining slices of bread.

2. Cut out sandwich shapes using cookie cutters. Place cookie cutter on top of sandwich; press down firmly. Remove excess trimmings.

3. Spread butter on both sides of sandwich. Heat large nonstick skillet over medium heat. Cook sandwiches 1 minute per side or until bread is golden and cheese melts.   *Makes 4 sandwiches*

Tip: Use 2½-inch star, heart, teddy bear or flower-shaped cookie cutters.

Prep Time: 15 minutes
Cook Time: 2 minutes

Grilled Cheese & Turkey Shapes

Super Sips
& Slurps

Serve up these cool and tasty punches and beverages at holiday and birthday parties or simply anytime you feel like making an ordinary day extra-special.

Creepy Crawler Punch

1 Creepy Crawler Ice Ring (recipe follows)
2 cups corn syrup
¼ cup water
6 cinnamon sticks
2 tablespoons whole cloves
½ teaspoon ground allspice
2 quarts (64 ounces) cranberry juice cocktail
1½ quarts (48 ounces) pineapple juice
1 quart (32 ounces) orange juice
½ cup lemon juice
2 liters (about 64 ounces) ginger ale

1. Prepare Creepy Crawler Ice Ring one day before serving. Freeze.

2. Cook and stir corn syrup and water in medium saucepan over medium-high heat. Add cinnamon sticks, cloves and allspice; stir gently. Bring to a boil; immediately reduce heat to a simmer. Simmer 10 minutes. Refrigerate, covered, until chilled. Remove cinnamon sticks and strain out cloves; discard.

3. Combine syrup mixture with juices and ginger ale in large punch bowl. Unmold Creepy Crawler Ice Ring by dipping bottom of mold briefly into hot water; add to punch bowl. *Makes 36 servings*

Creepy Crawler Ice Ring

1 cup gummy worms or other creepy crawler candy
1 liter (about 32 ounces) lemon-lime sports drink

Arrange gummy worms in bottom of 5-cup ring mold; fill mold with sports drink. Freeze until solid, 8 hours or overnight.

Makes 1 ice ring

Purple Cow Jumped Over the Moon

> 3 cups vanilla nonfat frozen yogurt
> 1 cup reduced-fat (2%) milk
> ½ cup thawed frozen grape juice concentrate (undiluted)
> 1½ teaspoons lemon juice

Place all ingredients in food processor or blender container; process until smooth. Serve immediately. *Makes 8 (½-cup) servings*

Razzmatazz Shake: Place 1 quart vanilla nonfat frozen yogurt, 1 cup vanilla nonfat yogurt and ¼ cup fat-free chocolate syrup in blender container; blend until smooth. Pour ½ of mixture evenly into 12 glasses; top with ½ of 12-ounce can root beer. Fill glasses equally with remaining yogurt mixture; top with remaining root beer. Makes 12 (⅔-cup) servings.

Sunshine Shake: Place 1 quart vanilla nonfat frozen yogurt, 1⅓ cups orange juice, 1 cup fresh or thawed frozen raspberries and 1 teaspoon sugar in blender container; blend until smooth. Pour into 10 glasses; sprinkle with ground nutmeg. Makes 10 (½-cup) servings.

Peanut Butter-Banana Shake

> 1 ripe banana, cut into chunks
> 2 tablespoons peanut butter
> ½ cup vanilla ice cream
> 1 cup milk

Place all ingredients in blender container. Cover; blend until smooth.

Makes about 2 cups

Purple Cow Jumped Over the Moon

Witches' Brew

> 2 cups apple cider
> 1½ to 2 cups vanilla ice cream
> 2 tablespoons honey
> ½ teaspoon ground cinnamon
> ¼ teaspoon ground nutmeg

Process cider, ice cream, honey, cinnamon and nutmeg in food processor or blender until smooth. Pour into glasses and sprinkle with additional nutmeg. Serve immediately.

Makes 4 (6-ounce) servings

Serving Suggestion: Add a few drops of desired food coloring to the ingredients in food processor to make a scary brew.

Hint: Reduce the fat in this tasty brew by replacing the vanilla ice cream with reduced-fat or fat-free ice cream or frozen yogurt.

Prep Time: 10 minutes

Quick Apple Punch

> 4 cups MOTT'S® Apple Juice
> 2 cups cranberry juice cocktail
> 2 tablespoons lemon juice
> 1 liter ginger ale, chilled
> Crushed ice, as needed

In large bowl, combine apple juice, cranberry juice and lemon juice. Fifteen minutes before serving, add ginger ale and crushed ice. Do not stir.

Makes 15 servings

Witches' Brew

Snowbird Mocktails

3 cups pineapple juice
1 can (14 ounces) sweetened condensed milk
1 can (6 ounces) frozen orange juice concentrate, thawed
½ teaspoon coconut extract
1 liter (about 32 ounces) ginger ale, chilled

1. Combine pineapple juice, sweetened condensed milk, orange juice concentrate and coconut extract in large pitcher; stir well. Cover; refrigerate at least 1 hour or up to 1 week.

2. To serve, pour ½ cup pineapple juice mixture into individual glasses (over crushed ice, if desired). Top off each glass with about ⅓ cup ginger ale. Garnish as desired. *Makes 10 servings*

Tip: Store unopened cans of sweetened condensed milk at room temperature for up to 6 months. Once opened, store them in an airtight container in the refrigerator for up to 5 days.

Prep Time: 10 minutes

"Moo-vin" Vanilla Milk Shake

1 pint (2 cups) low-fat sugar-free vanilla ice cream
½ cup fat-free (skim) milk
½ teaspoon vanilla
⅛ teaspoon decorator sprinkles (optional)

Combine all ingredients except decorator sprinkles in blender container. Cover; blend until smooth. Pour into 2 small glasses. Add decorator sprinkles, if desired. Serve immediately.

Makes 2 servings

26

Snowbird Mocktails

Sinister Slushies

4 bottles brightly colored sports drinks
4 to 8 ice cube trays

1. Pour each sports drink into separate ice cube tray; freeze overnight.

2. Place each color cubes into separate large resealable plastic food storage bags. Seal bags; crush cubes with rolling pin.

3. Layer different colors ice slush in clear glasses. Serve immediately with straws or spoons, if desired.

Makes 4 to 8 servings

Chocolate Syrup Soda

¼ cup cold club soda
3 tablespoons HERSHEY'S Syrup or HERSHEY'S
    Whoppers® Chocolate Malt Syrup
2 small scoops vanilla ice cream
    Additional club soda
    REDDI-WIP® Whipped Topping
    Maraschino cherry

• Combine soda and HERSHEY'S Syrup in tall glass; add ice cream. Fill glass with additional soda; stir gently.

• Top with REDDI-WIP® Whipped Topping and maraschino cherry.

Makes 1 serving

Double Chocolate Soda: Substitute chocolate ice cream for vanilla.

Sinister Slushies

Magic Potion

> **Creepy Crawler Ice Ring (page 21)**
> **1 cup boiling water**
> **2 packages (4-serving size each) lime-flavored gelatin**
> **3 cups cold water**
> **1½ liters (about 48 ounces) carbonated lemon-lime beverage, chilled**
> **½ cup superfine sugar**
> **Gummy worms (optional)**

1. Prepare Creepy Crawler Ice Ring one day before serving. Freeze.

2. Pour boiling water over gelatin in heatproof punch bowl; stir until gelatin dissolves. Stir in cold water. Add lemon-lime beverage and sugar; stir well (mixture will foam for several minutes).

3. Before serving, unmold ice ring by dipping bottom of mold briefly into hot water; add to punch bowl. Serve cups of punch garnished with gummy worms, if desired.   *Makes about 10 servings*

Super Suggestion!

Change this Magic Potion from creepy to cute. For the punch, use orange-flavored gelatin instead of lime. For the ice ring, use candy corn and candy pumpkins instead of gummy worms.

Magic Potion

Dripping Blood Punch

4 cups pineapple juice
1 cup orange juice
8 thick slices cucumber
2 cups ginger ale
   Ice
8 tablespoons grenadine syrup

1. Combine pineapple and orange juices in large pitcher. Refrigerate until ready to serve.

2. Cut cucumber slices into shape of vampire fangs (see photo). Stir ginger ale into chilled juice mixture. Fill glasses generously with ice. Pour punch over ice. Slowly drizzle 1 tablespoon grenadine over top of each serving. Garnish each glass with cucumber vampire fang.

Makes 8 servings

Mysterious Chocolate Mint Cooler

2 cups cold whole milk or half-and-half
¼ cup chocolate syrup
1 teaspoon peppermint extract
   Crushed ice
   Aerosol whipped topping
   Mint leaves

Combine milk, chocolate syrup and peppermint extract in small pitcher; stir until well blended. Fill 2 glasses with crushed ice. Pour chocolate-mint mixture over ice. Top with whipped topping. Garnish with mint leaves.

Makes about 2 (10-ounce) servings

Dripping Blood Punch

Make-'em-
Lite Bites

*Fun foods can be healthy, too! They're
silly, they're nutritious, and best of all . . .
your kids are going to love them.*

Little Piggy Pies

2 cups frozen mixed vegetables (carrots, potatoes, peas, celery, green beans, corn, onions and/or lima beans)
1 can (10¾ ounces) reduced-fat condensed cream of chicken soup, undiluted
8 ounces chopped cooked chicken
⅓ cup plain low-fat yogurt
⅓ cup water
½ teaspoon dried thyme leaves
¼ teaspoon poultry seasoning or ground sage
⅛ teaspoon garlic powder
1 tube (10 biscuits) refrigerated buttermilk biscuits

1. Preheat oven to 400°F.

2. Remove 10 green peas from frozen mixed vegetables. Combine remaining vegetables, soup, chicken, yogurt, water, thyme, poultry seasoning and garlic powder in medium saucepan. Bring to a boil, stirring frequently. Cover; keep warm.

3. Press five biscuits into 3-inch circles. Cut each remaining biscuit into eight wedges. Place two wedges on top of each circle; fold points down to form ears. Roll one wedge into small ball; place in center of each circle to form pig's snout. Use tip of spoon handle to make indents in snout for nostrils. Place 2 reserved green peas on each circle for eyes.

4. Spoon hot chicken mixture into 5 (10-ounce) custard cups. Place one biscuit pig on top of each. Place remaining biscuit wedges around each pig on top of chicken mixture, twisting one wedge tail for each. Bake 9 to 11 minutes or until biscuits are golden.

Makes 5 servings

Surfin' Salmon

⅓ **cup cornflake crumbs**
⅓ **cup cholesterol-free egg substitute**
2 **tablespoons fat-free (skim) milk**
¾ **teaspoon dried dill weed**
⅛ **teaspoon black pepper**
   Dash hot pepper sauce
1 **can (14½ ounces) salmon, drained and skin and bones removed**
   Nonstick cooking spray
1 **teaspoon olive oil**
6 **tablespoons tartar sauce**
5 **small pimiento pieces**

1. Combine cornflake crumbs, egg substitute, milk, dill weed, black pepper and hot pepper sauce in large mixing bowl. Add salmon; mix well.

2. Shape salmon mixture into 5 large egg-shaped balls. Flatten each into ¾-inch-thick oval. Pinch one end of each oval to make tail for each fish.

3. Spray large nonstick skillet with cooking spray. Add fish to skillet; cook 2 to 3 minutes over medium-high heat or until lightly browned. Turn fish over. Add oil to skillet. Continue cooking 2 to 3 minutes or until firm and lightly browned.

4. Place small drop tartar sauce and pimiento on each fish to make "eye." Serve with remaining tartar sauce, if desired.

Makes 5 servings

Tip: For a tasty side dish of sea plants, serve fish on a bed of shredded romaine lettuce and matchstick-size cucumber slices.

Surfin' Salmon

Sweet Treat Tortillas

   4 (7- to 8-inch) flour tortillas
   ½ package (4 ounces) Neufchâtel cheese, softened
   ¼ cup strawberry or other flavor spreadable fruit or
        preserves
   1 medium banana, peeled and chopped

1. Spread each tortilla with 1 ounce Neufchâtel cheese and
1 tablespoon spreadable fruit; top with ¼ of banana.

2. Roll up tortillas; cut crosswise into thirds.   *Makes 4 servings*

Tip: Substitute your favorite chopped fruit for banana.

Cinnamon-Spice Treats: Omit spreadable fruit and banana.
Mix small amounts of sugar, ground cinnamon and nutmeg, to taste,
into Neufchâtel cheese; spread evenly onto tortillas. Sprinkle lightly
with desired amount of chopped pecans or walnuts. Top with
chopped fruit, if desired; roll up. Cut crosswise into thirds. Makes
4 servings.

Frozen Fudge Pops

   ½ cup nonfat sweetened condensed milk
   ¼ cup unsweetened cocoa powder
   1¼ cups evaporated skimmed milk
   1 teaspoon vanilla

1. Beat sweetened condensed milk and cocoa in medium bowl. Add
evaporated milk and vanilla; beat until smooth.

2. Pour mixture into 8 small paper cups or 8 popsicle molds. Freeze
about 2 hours or until almost firm. Insert wooden popsicle stick into
center of each cup; freeze until solid.   *Makes 8 servings*

Sweet Treat Tortillas

Double-Sauced Chicken Pizza Bagels

1 whole bagel (about 3½ ounces), split in half
¼ cup prepared pizza sauce
½ cup diced cooked chicken breast
¼ cup (1 ounce) shredded part-skim mozzarella cheese
2 teaspoons grated Parmesan cheese

1. Place bagel halves on microwavable plate. Spread 1 tablespoon pizza sauce onto each bagel half.

2. Top each bagel half with ¼ cup chicken. Spoon 1 tablespoon pizza sauce over chicken on each bagel half.

3. Sprinkle 2 tablespoons mozzarella cheese over top of each bagel half.

4. Cover bagel halves loosely with waxed paper; microwave at HIGH 1 to 1½ minutes or until cheese melts.

5. Carefully remove waxed paper. Sprinkle each bagel half with 1 teaspoon Parmesan cheese. Let stand 1 minute before serving to cool slightly. (Bagels will be very hot.)   *Makes 2 servings*

Tip: For crunchier "pizzas," toast bagels before adding toppings.

Double-Sauced Chicken Pizza Bagel

Confetti Tuna in Celery Sticks

1 (3-ounce) pouch of STARKIST® Premium Albacore or
    Chunk Light Tuna
½ cup shredded red or green cabbage
½ cup shredded carrot
¼ cup shredded yellow squash or zucchini
3 tablespoons reduced-calorie cream cheese, softened
1 tablespoon plain low-fat yogurt
½ teaspoon dried basil, crushed
    Salt and pepper to taste
10 to 12 (4-inch) celery sticks, with leaves if desired

1. In a small bowl toss together tuna, cabbage, carrot and squash.

2. Stir in cream cheese, yogurt and basil. Add salt and pepper to taste.

3. With small spatula spread mixture evenly into celery sticks.

Makes 10 to 12 servings

Prep Time: 20 minutes

• • • • • • • • • • • • • • • • • • • •
What is the difference
between a fish and a piano?
• •
Answer: You can't tuna fish!

Confetti Tuna in Celery Sticks

Sloppy Joe's Bun Buggy

    4 hot dog buns (not split)
   16 thin slices cucumber or zucchini
   24 matchstick-size carrot strips, 1 inch long
    4 ripe olives or pimiento-stuffed olives
       Nonstick cooking spray
    1 (10-ounce) package 93% lean ground turkey
 1¼ cups prepared reduced-fat spaghetti sauce
   ½ cup chopped broccoli stems
    2 teaspoons prepared mustard
   ½ teaspoon Worcestershire sauce
       Dash salt
       Dash black pepper
    4 small pretzel twists

1. Hollow out hot dog buns. Use toothpick to make four holes in sides of each bun to attach "wheels." Use toothpick to make one hole in center of each cucumber slice; push carrot strip through hole. Press into holes in buns, making "wheels" on buns.

2. Cut each olive in half horizontally. Use toothpick to make two holes in one end of each bun to attach "headlights." Use carrot strips to attach olives to buns, making "headlights."

3. Spray large nonstick skillet with cooking spray. Cook and stir turkey in skillet over medium heat until no longer pink. Stir in spaghetti sauce, broccoli stems, mustard, Worcestershire, salt and pepper; heat through.

4. Spoon turkey mixture into hollowed-out buns. Press pretzel twist into ground turkey mixture, making "windshield" on each buggy.

Makes 4 servings

Sloppy Joe's Bun Buggy

One Potato, Two Potato

Nonstick cooking spray
2 medium baking potatoes, cut lengthwise into 4 wedges
Salt
½ cup unseasoned dry bread crumbs
2 tablespoons grated Parmesan cheese (optional)
1½ teaspoons dried oregano leaves, dill weed, Italian herbs
or paprika
Spicy brown or honey mustard, ketchup or reduced-fat
sour cream

1. Preheat oven to 425°F. Spray baking sheet with nonstick cooking spray; set aside.

2. Spray cut sides of potatoes generously with cooking spray; sprinkle lightly with salt.

3. Combine bread crumbs, Parmesan cheese, if desired, and oregano in shallow dish. Add potatoes; toss lightly until potatoes are generously coated with crumb mixture. Place on prepared baking sheet.

4. Bake 20 minutes or until potatoes are browned and tender. Serve warm with mustard for dipping.   *Makes 4 servings*

Potato Sweets: Omit bread crumbs, Parmesan cheese, oregano and mustard. Substitute sweet potatoes for baking potatoes. Cut and spray potatoes as directed; coat generously with desired amount of cinnamon-sugar in place of salt. Bake as directed. Serve warm with peach or pineapple preserves or honey mustard for dipping. Makes 4 servings.

One Potato, Two Potato

Super Nachos

12 large baked low-fat tortilla chips (about 1½ ounces)
½ cup (2 ounces) shredded reduced-fat Cheddar cheese
¼ cup fat-free refried beans
2 tablespoons chunky salsa

MICROWAVE DIRECTIONS

1. Arrange chips in single layer on large microwavable plate. Sprinkle cheese evenly over chips.

2. Spoon 1 teaspoon beans over each chip; top with ½ teaspoon salsa.

3. Microwave at MEDIUM (50% power) 1½ minutes; rotate dish. Microwave 1 to 1½ minutes or until cheese is melted.

Makes 2 servings

Conventional Directions: Preheat oven to 350°F. Substitute foil-covered baking sheet for microwavable plate. Assemble nachos on prepared baking sheet as directed above. Bake 10 to 12 minutes or until cheese is melted.

Tip: For a single serving of nachos, arrange 6 large tortilla chips on microwavable plate; top with ¼ cup cheese, 2 tablespoons refried beans and 1 tablespoon salsa. Microwave at MEDIUM (50% power) 1 minute; rotate dish. Microwave 30 seconds to 1 minute or until cheese is melted.

Super Nachos

Bread Pudding Snacks

1¼ cups reduced-fat (2%) milk

½ cup cholesterol-free egg substitute

⅓ cup sugar

1 teaspoon vanilla

⅛ teaspoon salt

⅛ teaspoon ground nutmeg (optional)

4 cups ½-inch cinnamon or cinnamon-raisin bread cubes (about 6 bread slices)

1 tablespoon margarine or butter, melted

1. Preheat oven to 350°F. Line 12 medium-size muffin cups with paper liners.

2. Combine milk, egg substitute, sugar, vanilla, salt and nutmeg, if desired, in medium bowl; mix well. Add bread; mix until well moistened. Let stand at room temperature 15 minutes.

3. Spoon bread mixture evenly into prepared cups; drizzle evenly with margarine.

4. Bake 30 to 35 minutes or until snacks are puffed and golden brown. Remove to wire rack to cool completely.

Makes 12 servings

Note: Snacks will puff up in the oven and fall slightly upon cooling.

Bread Pudding Snacks

Kids' Wraps

4 teaspoons Dijon honey mustard
2 (8-inch) fat-free flour tortillas
2 slices reduced-fat American cheese, cut in half
4 ounces thinly sliced fat-free oven-roasted turkey breast
½ cup shredded carrot (about 1 medium)
3 romaine lettuce leaves, washed and torn into bite-size pieces

1. Spread 2 teaspoons mustard evenly over 1 tortilla.

2. Top with 2 cheese halves, half of turkey, half of shredded carrot and half of torn lettuce.

3. Roll up tortilla; cut in half. Repeat with remaining ingredients.

Makes 2 servings

Snackin' Cinnamon Popcorn

3 to 4 teaspoons brown sugar substitute
1½ teaspoons salt
1½ teaspoons cinnamon
8 cups hot air-popped popcorn
Nonstick butter-flavored cooking spray

1. Combine brown sugar substitute, salt and cinnamon in small bowl; mix well.

2. Spread hot popped popcorn onto jelly-roll pan. Coat popcorn with cooking spray; immediately sprinkle cinnamon mixture over top. Serve immediately or store in container at room temperature up to 2 days.

Makes 4 servings

Kids' Wrap

Fruit Freezies

1½ cups (12 ounces) canned or thawed frozen peach slices, drained
¾ cup peach nectar
1 tablespoon sugar
¼ to ½ teaspoon coconut extract (optional)

1. Place peaches, nectar, sugar and extract, if desired, in food processor or blender container; process until smooth.

2. Spoon 2 tablespoons fruit mixture into each mold of ice cube tray.*

3. Freeze until almost firm. Insert frill pick into center of each cube; freeze until firm.   *Makes 12 servings*

Or, pour ⅓ cup fruit mixture into each of 8 plastic popsicle molds or small paper or plastic cups. Freeze until almost firm. Insert wooden stick into each mold; freeze until firm.

Apricot Freezies: Substitute canned apricot halves for peach slices and apricot nectar for peach nectar.

Pear Freezies: Substitute canned pear slices for peach slices, pear nectar for peach nectar and almond extract for coconut extract, if desired.

Pineapple Freezies: Substitute crushed pineapple for peach slices and unsweetened pineapple juice for peach nectar.

Mango Freezies: Substitute chopped fresh mango for peach slices and mango nectar for peach nectar. Omit coconut extract.

Fruit Freezies

Party Favor-ites

Children will be all smiles and giggles when you serve up these creative treats that are sure to be the hit of the party!

Chicken Nuggets with Barbecue Dipping Sauce

    1 pound boneless skinless chicken breasts
 ¼ cup all-purpose flour
 ¼ teaspoon salt
    Dash black pepper
    2 cups crushed reduced-fat baked cheese crackers
    1 teaspoon dried oregano leaves
    1 egg white
    1 tablespoon water
    3 tablespoons barbecue sauce
    2 tablespoons all-fruit peach or apricot jam

1. Preheat oven to 400°F. Rinse chicken. Pat dry with paper towels. Cut into 40 (1-inch) pieces.

2. Place flour, salt and pepper in large resealable plastic food storage bag. Combine cracker crumbs and oregano in shallow bowl. Whisk together egg white and water in small bowl.

3. Place 6 to 8 chicken pieces in bag with flour mixture; seal bag. Shake until chicken is well coated. Remove chicken from bag; shake off excess flour. Coat all sides of chicken pieces with egg white mixture. Roll in crumb mixture. Place in shallow baking pan. Repeat with remaining chicken pieces. Bake 10 to 13 minutes or until golden brown.

4. Meanwhile, combine barbecue sauce and jam in small saucepan. Cook and stir over low heat until heated through. Serve chicken nuggets with dipping sauce. *Makes 8 servings*

Silly Snake Sandwich

½ cup peanut butter

1 loaf (½ pound) sliced French or Italian bread, about
    11 inches long and 3 inches wide

1 *each* red bell pepper, black olive and green olive

½ cup jelly, any flavor

¼ cup marshmallow creme

1. Using small amount of peanut butter, attach first 2 inches (3 to 4 slices) bread loaf together to make snake head. Cut bell pepper into 2-inch-long tongue shape. Make very small horizontal slice in heel of bread, being careful not to cut all the way through. Place "tongue" into slice. Cut black olive in half lengthwise; attach with peanut butter to snake head for eyes. Cut 2 small pieces from green olive; attach with peanut butter for nostrils. Set snake head aside.

2. Combine remaining peanut butter, jelly and marshmallow creme in small bowl until smooth. Spread on half of bread slices; top with remaining bread slices.

3. Place snake head on large serving tray. Arrange sandwiches in wavy pattern to resemble slithering snake. Serve immediately.

Makes about 8 small sandwiches

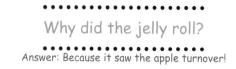

• • • • • • • • • • • • • • • • • •

Why did the jelly roll?

• • • • • • • • • • • • • • • • • •

Answer: Because it saw the apple turnover!

Silly Snake Sandwich

Ice Cream Cone Cupcakes

**1 package (18¼ ounces) white cake mix plus ingredients
to prepare**
2 tablespoons nonpareils
24 flat-bottomed ice cream cones
Vanilla and chocolate frosting
Candies and other decorations

1. Preheat oven to 350°F.

2. Prepare cake mix according to package directions. Stir in nonpareils.

3. Spoon ¼ cup batter into each ice cream cone.

4. Stand cones on cookie sheet. Bake 20 minutes or until toothpick inserted into center of cakes comes out clean. Cool on wire racks.

5. Frost each filled cone. Decorate as desired.

Makes 24 cupcakes

These cupcakes are best when served the day they are prepared. Store them loosely covered.

Ice Cream Cone Cupcakes

Monster Mouths

1 teaspoon vegetable oil

1 medium onion, chopped

4 slices bacon, chopped

1 pound ground beef

2 medium plum tomatoes, seeded and chopped

½ teaspoon salt

¼ teaspoon black pepper

4 slices American cheese, chopped

½ (12-ounce) package jumbo pasta shells (about 18 shells), cooked and drained

Baby carrots, olives, red bell pepper, small pickles and cheese slices for decoration

1. Preheat oven to 350°F. Lightly grease 13×9-inch baking dish. Heat oil in large skillet over medium heat. Add onion and bacon; cook until onion is tender. Add beef; cook and stir about 5 minutes or until beef is no longer pink. Stir in tomatoes, salt and black pepper. Stir in chopped cheese. Spoon mixture into cooked shells; place in prepared baking dish.

2. Cut carrot into very thin strips. Cut small slit in each olive; poke one end of thin carrot strip in olive for eyes. Cut red bell pepper into fang shapes. Slice pickles lengthwise to make tongue shapes. Cut cheese slice into zig-zag pattern for teeth. Set aside.

3. Bake stuffed shells 3 to 5 minutes or until hot; remove from oven. Decorate as desired with eyes, fangs, tongues and teeth. Serve immediately. *Makes about 6 servings*

Monster Mouths

Pizza Snack Cups

1 can (12 ounces) refrigerated biscuits (10 biscuits)
½ pound ground beef
1 jar (14 ounces) RAGÚ® Pizza Quick® Sauce
½ cup shredded mozzarella cheese (about 2 ounces)

1. Preheat oven to 375°F. In muffin pan, evenly press each biscuit in bottom and up side of each cup; chill until ready to fill.

2. In 10-inch skillet, brown ground beef over medium-high heat; drain. Stir in Ragú Pizza Quick Sauce and heat through.

3. Evenly spoon beef mixture into prepared muffin cups. Bake 15 minutes. Sprinkle with cheese; bake an additional 5 minutes or until cheese is melted and biscuits are golden. Let stand 5 minutes. Gently remove pizza cups from muffin pan; serve.

Makes 10 pizza cups

Prep Time: 10 minutes
Cook Time: 25 minutes

• •
What did the computer order
at the restaurant?
• • • • • • • • • • • • • • • •
Answer: A byte!

Pizza Snack Cups

Quick Sand

¾ cup creamy peanut butter
5 ounces cream cheese, softened
1 cup (8 ounces) pineapple preserves
⅓ cup milk
1 teaspoon Worcestershire sauce
Dash hot pepper sauce (optional)
1 can (6 breadsticks) refrigerated breadstick dough
5 rich round crackers, crushed
Cut-up vegetables such as carrots and celery, or fruit
such as apples and pears, for dipping

1. Combine peanut butter and cream cheese in large bowl until well blended. Stir in preserves, milk, Worcestershire sauce and hot pepper sauce, if desired. Transfer to serving bowl or spread in 8- or 9-inch glass pie plate. Cover with plastic wrap; refrigerate until ready to serve.

2. Preheat oven to 375°F. Cut each breadstick in half crosswise; place on ungreased baking sheet. Make 3 slits in one short end of each breadstick half to resemble fingers. Cut small piece of dough from other short end; press dough piece into "hand" to resemble thumb. Bake 8 to 10 minutes or until golden brown.

3. Just before serving, sprinkle dip with cracker crumbs; serve with breadstick hands, vegetables and fruit. Garnish as desired.

Makes 12 to 16 servings

Quick Sand

Swampy Thing

1 (1½-gallon) unused glass fish bowl
1 large package (8-serving size) *or* 2 packages (4-serving
   size each) yellow gelatin dessert
1 small package (4-serving size) yellow gelatin dessert
1 small package (4-serving size) blue gelatin dessert
1 can (11 ounces) fruit cocktail, drained
   Curly endive sprigs
   Plastic toy skeleton
   Plastic toy tire or car

1. Wash and rinse unused fish bowl. Set aside to dry.

2. Prepare gelatin desserts according to package directions, mixing colors to make a swampy green. Pour into clean fish bowl.

3. Slowly pour in drained fruit cocktail, letting it sink to bottom of fish bowl. Chill in refrigerator 1 hour or until set but not firm.

4. Remove from refrigerator. Place endive in gelatin, using chopstick or knife to push to bottom. Using same technique, add skeleton, tire and candies to create swamp. Return fish bowl to refrigerator until gelatin is set.   *Makes 6 to 8 servings*

Note: Be sure to remove any plastic toys or inedible items before serving.

Swampy Thing

Perfect Pita Pizzas

2 whole wheat or white pita bread rounds
½ cup spaghetti or pizza sauce
¾ cup (3 ounces) shredded part-skim mozzarella cheese
1 small zucchini, sliced ¼ inch thick
½ small carrot, peeled and sliced
2 cherry tomatoes, halved
¼ small green bell pepper, sliced

1. Preheat oven to 375°F. Line baking sheet with foil; set aside.

2. Using small scissors, carefully split each pita around edge; separate to form 2 rounds.

3. Place rounds, rough sides up, on prepared baking sheet. Bake 5 minutes.

4. Spread 2 tablespoons sauce onto each round; sprinkle with cheese. Decorate with vegetables to create faces. Bake 10 to 12 minutes or until cheese melts.   *Makes 4 servings*

Pepperoni Pita Pizzas: Prepare pita rounds, partially bake and top with sauce and cheese as directed. Place 2 small pepperoni slices on each pizza for eyes. Decorate with cut-up fresh vegetables for rest of face. Continue to bake as directed.

• •

Why does a Mexican weather
report make you hungry?

• •
Answer: Because it's chili today and hot tamale!

Perfect Pita Pizzas

Chocolate Peanut Butter Fondue

⅓ cup sugar
⅓ cup unsweetened cocoa powder
⅓ cup low-fat (1%) milk
3 tablespoons light corn syrup
2 tablespoons reduced-fat peanut butter
½ teaspoon vanilla
2 medium apples, cored and sliced
2 medium bananas, cut into 1-inch pieces
16 large strawberries

1. Combine sugar, cocoa, milk, corn syrup and peanut butter in medium saucepan. Cook, stirring constantly, over medium heat until hot. Remove from heat; stir in vanilla.

2. Pour fondue into medium serving bowl; serve warm or at room temperature with fruit for dipping.   *Makes 8 servings*

Super Suggestion!

Kids will enjoy eating fruit with this fondue! Mix and match various types. Orange sections, pear slices and fresh raspberries are just a few of the many other kinds of fruit you can serve with this sweet chocolate treat.

Chocolate Peanut Butter Fondue

Sea Serpents

1 package (8 rolls) crescent dinner rolls
Fruit-flavored cereal rings
1 egg, beaten
Sunflower seeds, sesame seeds and poppy seeds
1 can (6 ounces) water-packed tuna, drained
Mayonnaise
Pimiento strips (optional)
Parsley (optional)

1. Separate dough into triangles. Press each triangle into serpent shape, with thin tapered tail and wider head, on baking sheet. Head should be about ¼ inch thick.

2. Press cereal rings onto heads for eyes. Brush dough serpents with egg; sprinkle with choice of seeds. Bake according to crescent roll package directions.

3. Remove from oven to wire racks; cool. Slice head end lengthwise to form mouth. Mix tuna with mayonnaise to taste. Fill mouth with tuna mixture. Add pimiento strips for tongues, if desired. Garnish with parsley, if desired, for seaweed.   *Makes 8 servings*

Super Suggestion!

If your child won't eat tuna, fill the mouths of these hungry creatures with peanut butter, egg salad, chicken salad or strips of cold cuts and cheese instead.

Sea Serpents

Octo-Dogs and Shells

4 refrigerated hot dogs
1½ cups uncooked small shell pasta
1½ cups frozen mixed vegetables
1 cup prepared Alfredo sauce
Prepared yellow mustard in squeeze bottle
Cheese-flavored fish-shaped crackers

1. Lay 1 hot dog on cutting surface. Starting 1 inch from one end of hot dog, slice vertically in half. Roll hot dog ¼ turn. Starting 1 inch from same end, slice in half vertically again, making 4 segments connected at top. Slice each segment in half vertically, creating a total of 8 "legs." Repeat with remaining hot dogs.

2. Place hot dogs in medium saucepan; cover with water. Bring to a boil over medium-high heat. Remove from heat; set aside.

3. Prepare pasta according to package directions, stirring in vegetables during last 3 minutes of cooking time. Drain; return to pan. Stir in Alfredo sauce. Heat over low heat until heated through. Divide pasta mixture between 4 plates.

4. Drain octo-dogs. Arrange one octo-dog on top of pasta mixture on each plate. Draw faces on "heads" of octo-dogs with mustard. Sprinkle crackers over pasta. *Makes 4 servings*

• • • • • • • • • • • • • • • • • • •

What is the worst thing about being an octopus?

• • • • • • • • • • • • • • • • • • •
Answer: Having to wash your hands before dinner!

Octo-Dog and Shells

Hooray for Holidays!

Children cherish holidays. Here are some festive treats that will give them yet one more reason to look forward to these special days.

Valentine Surprise

Pink and white decorating icings
18 whole plain graham crackers or chocolate-flavored graham crackers
6 scoops (about ½ cup each) strawberry-flavored ice cream or frozen yogurt
Assorted valentine candies, jelly beans or small fresh flowers

1. Spoon icings into pastry bags fitted with decorating tips;* set aside.

2. Break graham crackers crosswise in half. Place 1 scoop ice cream in center of each of 6 graham cracker halves.

3. To form sides of each box, stand up 1 graham cracker half along each of the 4 sides of each graham cracker half topped with ice cream; pipe icing along seams to secure. Top boxes with 6 graham cracker halves; pipe icing along remaining seams to secure.

4. Place boxes in freezer; freeze ½ hour. Remove boxes to work surface. Decorate boxes as desired with icing and candies, using icing to secure candies to boxes. Freeze until ready to serve.

Makes 6 servings

Or, place icing in small resealable plastic food storage bag. Cut tiny hole in corner of bag.

Shamrock Ice Cream Sandwiches

Butter Cookie Dough (page 82)
Green food coloring
1 pint (2 cups) ice cream or frozen yogurt, any flavor

1. Prepare cookie dough; tint desired shade with food coloring. Wrap in plastic wrap; refrigerate until firm, about 4 hours or overnight.

2. Preheat oven to 350°F.

3. Roll out dough on lightly floured surface to ¼-inch thickness. Cut dough using 3½- to 5-inch shamrock-shaped cookie cutter. Gather and reroll scraps to make 12 to 16 cut-outs. Place on ungreased cookie sheets.

4. Bake 8 to 10 minutes or until cookies are lightly browned around edges. Remove cookies to wire racks; cool completely.

5. Remove ice cream from freezer; let stand at room temperature 10 minutes to slightly soften. Spread 4 to 5 tablespoons ice cream onto flat sides of ½ the cookies. Place remaining cookies, flat sides down, on ice cream; press cookies together lightly.

6. Wrap each sandwich in foil; freeze until firm, about 2 hours or overnight. *Makes 6 to 8 cookie sandwiches*

Note: Filled cookies store well up to 1 week in freezer.

Valentine Ice Cream Sandwiches: Prepare, tint and chill cookie dough as directed, substituting red food coloring for green food coloring. Cut dough with heart-shaped cookie cutter. Continue as directed.

continued on page 82

Shamrock Ice Cream Sandwiches

Shamrock Ice Cream Sandwiches, continued

Patriotic Ice Cream Sandwiches: Prepare and chill cookie dough as directed. Divide dough in half. Tint ½ of dough with red food coloring and ½ of dough with blue food coloring, substituting for green food coloring. Cut dough with star-shaped cookie cutter. Continue as directed, making each sandwich with 1 red and 1 blue cookie.

Pumpkin Ice Cream Sandwiches: Prepare, tint and chill cookie dough as directed, substituting orange food coloring for green food coloring. Cut dough with pumpkin-shaped cookie cutter. Continue as directed.

Christmas Tree Ice Cream Sandwiches: Prepare, tint and chill cookie dough as directed. Cut dough with Christmas tree-shaped cookie cutter. Continue as directed.

Butter Cookie Dough

> ¾ cup (1½ sticks) butter, softened
> ¼ cup granulated sugar
> ¼ cup packed light brown sugar
> 1 egg yolk
> 1¾ cups all-purpose flour
> ¾ teaspoon baking powder
> ⅛ teaspoon salt

Combine butter, granulated sugar, brown sugar and egg yolk in medium bowl. Beat at medium speed of electric mixer until well blended. Add flour, baking powder and salt; mix well.

Easter Egg Baskets

8 (6-inch) flour tortillas, divided
4 tablespoons butter, melted and divided
4 bacon slices, cut into 1-inch pieces
½ cup chopped green bell pepper
½ cup chopped red bell pepper
3 tablespoons chopped onion
4 eggs
3 tablespoons milk
¼ teaspoon salt
¼ teaspoon hot pepper sauce
⅛ teaspoon black pepper

1. Preheat oven to 350°F.

2. Brush 6 tortillas with melted butter; let stand until pliable, about 5 minutes. Gently ease buttered tortillas into 6 small custard cups.

3. For handles, cut each of 2 remaining tortillas into 3 (1-inch) strips (to make 6 strips total). Brush strips with remaining butter. Invert 6-cup muffin pan. Place 1 tortilla strip around bottom of each cup. Bake tortilla baskets and handles 10 to 15 minutes or until golden brown. Remove baskets and handles to wire rack; cool.

4. Meanwhile, cook bacon in medium skillet over medium-high heat until crisp, stirring occasionally. Remove bacon from skillet; set aside. Pour off all but 1 tablespoon bacon fat from skillet. Add bell peppers and onion to skillet; cook and stir until crisp-tender.

5. Whisk together eggs, milk, salt, hot pepper sauce and black pepper. Add to vegetable mixture in skillet; cook and stir until eggs are set. Stir in bacon. Divide egg mixture evenly among 6 prepared baskets. Place 1 handle in each basket. Serve warm.

Makes 6 servings

Springtime Nests

1 cup butterscotch chips
½ cup light corn syrup
½ cup creamy peanut butter
⅓ cup sugar
2 cups cornflakes, slightly crushed
2½ cups chow mein noodles
Jelly beans or malted milk egg candies

1. Combine butterscotch chips, corn syrup, peanut butter and sugar in large microwavable bowl. Microwave at HIGH 1 to 1½ minutes or until melted and smooth, stirring at 30-second intervals.

2. Stir in cornflakes and chow mein noodles until evenly coated. Shape scant ¼-cupfuls mixture into balls; make indentation in centers to make nests. Place nests on waxed paper to set. Place 3 jelly beans in each nest.   *Makes 1½ dozen cookies*

The Red, White and Blue Sundae

Strawberry ice cream
Slice of pound cake
HERSHEY'S Strawberry Syrup
REDDI-WIP® Whipped Topping
Fresh blueberries

• Place scoop of ice cream on top of pound cake; drizzle with HERSHEY'S Strawberry Syrup.

• Top with REDDI-WIP® Whipped Topping and blueberries.

Makes 1 serving

84

Springtime Nests

Color-Bright Ice Cream Sandwiches

¾ cup (1½ sticks) butter or margarine, softened
¾ cup creamy peanut butter
1¼ cups firmly packed light brown sugar
1 large egg
1 teaspoon vanilla extract
1½ cups all-purpose flour
1 teaspoon baking soda
¼ teaspoon salt
1¾ cups "M&M's"® Chocolate Mini Baking Bits, divided
2 quarts vanilla or chocolate ice cream, slightly softened

Preheat oven to 350°F. In large bowl cream butter, peanut butter and sugar until light and fluffy; beat in egg and vanilla. In medium bowl combine flour, baking soda and salt; blend into creamed mixture. Stir in 1⅓ cups "M&M's"® Chocolate Mini Baking Bits. Shape dough into 1¼-inch balls. Place about 2 inches apart on ungreased cookie sheets. Gently flatten to about ½-inch thickness with fingertips. Place 7 or 8 of the remaining "M&M's"® Chocolate Mini Baking Bits on each cookie; press in lightly. Bake 10 to 12 minutes or until edges are light brown. *Do not overbake.* Cool about 1 minute on cookie sheets; cool completely on wire racks. Assemble cookies in pairs with about ⅓ cup ice cream; press cookies together lightly. Wrap each sandwich in plastic wrap; freeze until firm. *Makes about 24 ice cream sandwiches*

Color-Bright Ice Cream Sandwiches

Hidden Pumpkin Pies

1½ **cups canned solid-pack pumpkin**
1 **cup evaporated skimmed milk**
½ **cup cholesterol-free egg substitute** *or* **2 eggs**
¼ **cup granular sucralose-based sugar substitute or granulated sugar**
1 **teaspoon pumpkin pie spice***
1¼ **teaspoons vanilla, divided**
3 **egg whites**
¼ **teaspoon cream of tartar**
⅓ **cup honey**

*Substitute ½ teaspoon ground cinnamon, ¼ teaspoon ground ginger and ⅛ teaspoon each ground allspice and ground nutmeg for 1 teaspoon pumpkin pie spice, if desired.

1. Preheat oven to 350°F.

2. Combine pumpkin, evaporated milk, egg substitute, sugar substitute, pumpkin pie spice and 1 teaspoon vanilla in large bowl. Pour into 6 (6-ounce) custard cups or 6 (¾-cup) soufflé dishes. Place in shallow baking dish or pan. Pour boiling water around custard cups to depth of 1 inch. Bake 25 minutes.

3. Meanwhile, beat egg whites, cream of tartar and remaining ¼ teaspoon vanilla at high speed of electric mixer until soft peaks form. Gradually add honey, beating until stiff peaks form.

4. Spread egg white mixture over tops of hot pumpkin pies. Return to oven. Bake 15 to 16 minutes or until tops of pies are golden brown. Let stand 10 minutes. Serve warm.   *Makes 6 servings*

Hidden Pumpkin Pie

Indian Corn

¼ cup (½ stick) butter or margarine
1 package (10.5 ounces) mini marshmallows
   Yellow food coloring
8 cups peanut butter and chocolate puffed corn cereal
1 cup candy-coated chocolate pieces, divided
10 lollipop sticks
   Tan and green raffia

1. Line large baking sheet with waxed paper; set aside.

2. Melt butter in large heavy saucepan over low heat. Add marshmallows; stir until melted and smooth. Tint with food coloring until desired shade is reached. Add cereal and ½ cup chocolate pieces; stir until evenly coated. Remove from heat.

3. With lightly greased hands, quickly divide mixture into 10 oblong pieces. Push lollipop stick halfway into each piece; shape like ear of corn. Place on prepared baking sheet. Press remaining ½ cup chocolate pieces into each "ear." Let stand until set.

4. Tie or tape raffia to lollipop sticks to resemble corn husks.

Makes 10 servings

Super Suggestion!

Lollipop sticks and colored raffia are sold at craft and hobby stores.

Indian Corn

Yummy Mummy Cookies

⅔ cup butter or margarine, softened
1 cup sugar
2 teaspoons vanilla extract
2 eggs
2½ cups all-purpose flour
½ cup HERSHEY'S Cocoa
½ teaspoon salt
¼ teaspoon baking soda
1 cup HERSHEY'S MINI CHIPS™ Semi-Sweet Chocolate Chips
1 to 2 packages (10 ounces each) HERSHEY'S Premier White Chips
1 to 2 tablespoons shortening (do *not* use butter, margarine, spread or oil)
Additional HERSHEY'S MINI CHIPS™ Semi-Sweet Chocolate Chips

1. Beat butter, sugar and vanilla in large bowl until creamy. Add eggs; beat well. Stir together flour, cocoa, salt and baking soda; gradually add to butter mixture, beating until blended. Stir in 1 cup small chocolate chips. Refrigerate dough 15 to 20 minutes or until firm enough to handle.

2. Heat oven to 350°F.

3. To form mummy body, using 1 tablespoon dough, roll into 3½-inch carrot shape; place on ungreased cookie sheet. To form head, using 1 teaspoon dough, roll into ball the size and shape of a grape; press onto wide end of body. Repeat procedure with remaining dough.

4. Bake 8 to 9 minutes or until set. Cool slightly; remove from cookie sheet to wire rack. Cool completely.

continued on page 94

Yummy Mummy Cookies

Yummy Mummy Cookies, continued

5. Place 1⅔ cups (10-ounce package) white chips and 1 tablespoon shortening in microwave-safe pie plate or shallow bowl. Microwave at HIGH (100%) 1 minute; stir until chips are melted.

6. Coat tops of cookies by placing one cookie at a time on table knife or narrow metal spatula; spoon white chip mixture evenly over cookie to coat. (If mixture begins to thicken, return to microwave for a few seconds). Place coated cookies on wax paper. Melt additional chips with shortening, if needed, for additional coating. As coating begins to set on cookies, using a toothpick, score lines and facial features into coating to resemble mummy. Place 2 small chocolate chips on each cookie for eyes. Store, covered, in cool, dry place.

Makes about 30 cookies

Dem Bones

   1 package (6 ounces) sliced ham
   ¾ cup (3 ounces) shredded Swiss cheese
   ½ cup mayonnaise
   1 tablespoon sweet pickle relish
   ½ teaspoon mustard
   ¼ teaspoon black pepper
   6 slices white bread

1. Place ham in bowl of food processor or blender; process until ground. Combine ham, cheese, mayonnaise, relish, mustard and pepper in small bowl until well blended.

2. Cut out 12 bone shapes from bread using 3½-inch bone-shaped cookie cutter or sharp knife. Spread half of "bones" with 2 tablespoons ham mixture; top with remaining "bones."

Makes 6 sandwiches

Trick-or-Treat Pizza Biscuits

1 can (8 biscuits) refrigerated jumbo biscuits
3 tablespoons prepared pizza sauce
   Assorted pizza toppings: cooked crumbled Italian
      sausage, pepperoni slices, sliced mushrooms and/or
      black olives
½ cup (2 ounces) shredded pizza-blend or mozzarella
   cheese
1 egg yolk
1 teaspoon water
   Assorted food colorings

1. Preheat oven to 375°F.

2. Press 4 biscuits into 4-inch rounds on ungreased baking sheet. Spread center of each biscuit with about 2 teaspoons pizza sauce. Place 4 to 5 pepperoni slices on each biscuit; top with 2 tablespoons cheese. Press remaining 4 biscuits into 4-inch rounds and place over cheese; press edges together to seal. Press design into top of each biscuit with Halloween cookie cutter, being careful not to cut all the way through top biscuit.

3. Combine egg yolk and water in small bowl. Divide yolk mixture among several small bowls. Tint each with food colorings. Decorate Halloween imprints with egg yolk paints using small, clean craft paintbrushes. Bake 12 to 15 minutes or until biscuits are golden brown at edges.   *Makes 4 servings*

Note: This recipe tastes best when made with regular biscuits instead of butter-flavored biscuits.

Snowmen

1 package (20 ounces) refrigerated chocolate chip
    cookie dough
1½ cups sifted powdered sugar
2 tablespoons milk
    Candy corn, gumdrops, chocolate chips, licorice and
    other assorted small candies

1. Preheat oven to 375°F. Remove dough from wrapper. Cut dough into 12 equal sections. Divide each section into 3 balls: small, medium and large.

2. For each snowman, place 1 *each* small, medium and large balls ¼ inch apart on ungreased cookie sheet.

3. Bake 10 to 12 minutes or until edges are very lightly browned. Cool 4 minutes on cookie sheets. Remove to wire racks; cool completely.

4. Mix powdered sugar and milk in medium bowl until smooth. Pour glaze evenly over cookies. Let cookies stand 20 minutes or until set.

5. Decorate with assorted candies to create faces, hats, scarves and arms.

Makes 1 dozen cookies

. . . .

Why did the cookie go
to the doctor's office?

. . . .
Answer: Because he was feeling crummy!

Snowmen

Yuletide Twisters

1 (6-ounce) package white baking bars
4 teaspoons fat-free (skim) milk
4 teaspoons light corn syrup
8 ounces reduced-salt pretzel twists (about 80)
  Assorted sprinkles, cookie decorations or colored sugar

1. Line baking sheet with waxed paper; set aside.

2. Melt baking bars in small saucepan over low heat, stirring constantly. Stir in skim milk and corn syrup. Do not remove saucepan from heat.

3. Holding pretzel with fork, dip 1 side of pretzel into melted mixture to coat. Place coated side up on prepared baking sheet; immediately sprinkle with desired decorations. Repeat with remaining pretzels. Refrigerate 15 to 20 minutes or until firm.

Makes 10 servings

Chocolate Twisters: Substitute 1 cup semisweet chocolate chips for white baking bars.

Caramel Dippity Do's: Heat 1 cup fat-free caramel sauce and ⅓ cup finely chopped pecans in small saucepan over low heat until warm. Pour into small serving bowl. Serve with pretzels for dipping. Makes 8 servings (about 2 tablespoons each).

Chocolate Dippity Do's: Heat 1 cup fat-free hot fudge sauce and ⅓ cup finely chopped pecans or walnuts in small saucepan over low heat until warm. Pour into small serving bowl. Serve with pretzels for dipping. Makes 8 servings (about 2 tablespoons each).

Yuletide Twisters

Extreme Sweets

Any child's sweet tooth is sure to be satisfied with these delectable treats. Bears, turtles, lady bugs and flowers are just a few fun shapes of these sweeter-than-sweet treats.

Cookie Crumb Sundae

1 package (about 18 ounces) chocolate creme-filled sandwich cookies
4 cups milk, divided
1 package (4-serving size) cheesecake-flavored instant pudding mix
1 package (4-serving size) chocolate fudge-flavored instant pudding mix
1 container (8 ounces) frozen whipped topping, thawed
12 to 16 maraschino cherries, drained

1. Place cookies in large resealable plastic food storage bag; crush with rolling pin. Place ¾ of crumbs in bottom of 13×9-inch baking pan or large serving bowl.

2. Combine 2 cups milk and cheesecake-flavored pudding mix in large bowl. Prepare according to package directions. Pour pudding evenly over cookie crumbs.

3. Repeat with remaining 2 cups milk and chocolate fudge-flavored pudding mix. Pour evenly over cheesecake pudding.

4. Spread whipped topping over pudding. Sprinkle remaining cookie crumbs over whipped topping. Top with maraschino cherries. Chill 1 hour before serving.   *Makes 12 to 14 servings*

Tip: For birthday parties, holidays and picnics, make this dessert in individual disposable plastic cups. Decorate with festive colored sprinkles.

Mice Creams

1 pint vanilla ice cream
1 (4-ounce) package READY CRUST® Mini-Graham Cracker
   Pie Crusts
   Ears—12 KEEBLER® Grasshopper® cookies
   Tails—3 chocolate twigs, broken in half *or* 6 (3-inch)
      pieces black shoestring licorice
   Eyes and noses—18 brown candy-coated chocolate
      candies
   Whiskers—2 teaspoons chocolate sprinkles

1. Place 1 scoop vanilla ice cream into each crust. Press cookie
ears and tails into ice cream. Press eyes, noses, and whiskers in
place. Serve immediately. Do not refreeze.   *Makes 6 servings*

Prep Time: 15 minutes

Mini Pizza Cookies

1 tube (20 ounces) refrigerated sugar cookie dough
2 cups (16 ounces) prepared pink frosting
   "M&M's"® Chocolate Mini Baking Bits
   Variety of additional toppings such as shredded coconut,
      granola, raisins, nuts, small pretzels, snack mixes,
      sunflower seeds, popped corn and mini marshmallows

Preheat oven to 350°F. Lightly grease cookie sheets; set aside.
Divide dough into 8 equal portions. On lightly floured surface, roll
each portion of dough into ¼-inch-thick circle; place circles about
2 inches apart on prepared cookie sheets. Bake 10 to 13 minutes or
until golden brown on edges. Cool completely on wire racks. Spread
top of each pizza with frosting; sprinkle with "M&M's"® Chocolate
Mini Baking Bits and 2 or 3 suggested toppings.

Makes 8 cookies

Mice Creams

Snackin' Banana Split

1 small ripe banana, peeled

1 small scoop vanilla fat-free or low-fat frozen yogurt (about 3 tablespoons)

1 small scoop strawberry fat-free or low-fat frozen yogurt (about 3 tablespoons)

⅓ cup sliced fresh strawberries or blueberries

2 tablespoons all-fruit strawberry fruit spread

1 teaspoon hot water

2 tablespoons low-fat granola cereal

1 maraschino cherry (optional)

1. Split banana in half lengthwise. Place in shallow bowl; top with frozen yogurt and strawberries.

2. Combine fruit spread and water in small bowl; mix well. Spoon over yogurt; sprinkle with granola. Top with cherry, if desired.

Makes 1 serving

• •

What did the banana do when
it heard the ice scream?

• • • • • • • • • • • • • • • • • • • •
Answer: It split!

Snackin' Banana Split

Brownie Turtle Cookies

2 squares (1 ounce each) unsweetened baking chocolate

⅓ cup solid vegetable shortening

1 cup granulated sugar

2 large eggs

½ teaspoon vanilla extract

1¼ cups all-purpose flour

½ teaspoon baking powder

½ teaspoon salt

1 cup "M&M's"® Milk Chocolate Mini Baking Bits, divided

1 cup pecan halves

⅓ cup caramel ice cream topping

⅓ cup shredded coconut

⅓ cup finely chopped pecans

Preheat oven to 350°F. Lightly grease cookie sheets; set aside. Heat chocolate and shortening in 2-quart saucepan over low heat, stirring constantly until melted; remove from heat. Mix in sugar, eggs and vanilla. Blend in flour, baking powder and salt. Stir in ⅔ cup "M&M's"® Milk Chocolate Mini Baking Bits. For each cookie, arrange 3 pecan halves, with ends almost touching at center, on prepared cookie sheets. Drop dough by rounded teaspoonfuls onto center of each group of pecans; mound the dough slightly. Bake 8 to 10 minutes or just until set. *Do not overbake.* Cool completely on wire racks. In small bowl combine ice cream topping, coconut and chopped nuts; top each cookie with about 1½ teaspoons mixture. Press remaining ⅓ cup "M&M's"® Milk Chocolate Mini Baking Bits into topping.   *Makes about 2½ dozen cookies*

Brownie Turtle Cookies

Lady Bugs

¾ **cup shortening**
½ **cup sugar**
¼ **cup honey**
 1 **egg**
½ **teaspoon vanilla**
 2 **cups all-purpose flour**
⅓ **cup cornmeal**
 1 **teaspoon baking powder**
½ **teaspoon salt**
   Orange and black icings
   Miniature yellow candy-coated chocolate pieces

1. Beat shortening, sugar and honey in large bowl at medium speed of electric mixer until light and fluffy. Add egg and vanilla; beat until well blended. Combine flour, cornmeal, baking powder and salt in medium bowl. Add to shortening mixture; mix at low speed until blended. Shape dough into disc. Wrap in plastic wrap; refrigerate 2 hours or overnight.

2. Preheat oven to 375°F. Divide dough into 24 equal pieces. Shape each piece into 2×1¼-inch oval-shaped ball. Place balls 2 inches apart on ungreased cookie sheets.

3. Bake 10 to 12 minutes or until lightly browned. Cool on cookie sheets 2 minutes. Remove to wire racks; cool completely.

4. Decorate cookies with orange and black icings and candy-coated pieces to resemble lady bugs. *Makes 2 dozen cookies*

Lady Bugs

Mud Cups

1 package (18 ounces) refrigerated sugar cookie dough
¼ cup unsweetened cocoa powder
3 containers (4 ounces each) prepared chocolate pudding
1¼ cups chocolate sandwich cookie crumbs (about 15 cookies)
    Gummy worms

1. Preheat oven to 350°F. Grease 18 (2½- or 2¾-inch) muffin pan cups.

2. Remove dough from wrapper; place in large bowl. Let dough stand at room temperature about 15 minutes.

3. Add cocoa to dough; beat at medium speed of electric mixer until well blended. Shape dough into 18 balls; press onto bottoms and up sides of prepared muffin cups.

4. Bake 12 to 14 minutes or until set. Remove from oven; gently press down center of each cookie with back of teaspoon. Cool in pan 10 minutes. Remove cups from pan; cool completely on wire racks.

5. Fill each cup with 1 to 2 tablespoons pudding; sprinkle with cookie crumbs. Garnish with gummy worms.

Makes 1½ dozen cookie cups

Mud Cups

Peanut Butter Bears

2 cups uncooked quick oats
2 cups all-purpose flour
1 tablespoon baking powder
1 cup granulated sugar
¾ cup (1½ sticks) butter, softened
½ cup creamy peanut butter
½ cup packed brown sugar
½ cup cholesterol-free egg substitute *or* 2 eggs
1 teaspoon vanilla
3 tablespoons miniature chocolate chips

1. Combine oats, flour and baking powder; set aside.

2. Beat granulated sugar, butter, peanut butter and brown sugar in large bowl at medium-high speed of electric mixer until well blended. Add egg substitute and vanilla; beat until light and fluffy. Add oat mixture; beat at low speed until combined. Wrap dough in plastic wrap; refrigerate 1 to 2 hours or until easy to handle.

3. Preheat oven to 375°F.

4. For each bear, shape 1 (1-inch) ball for body and 1 (¾-inch) ball for head. Place body and head together on baking sheet; flatten slightly. Make 7 small balls for arms, legs, nose and ears. Place on bear body and head. Place 2 chocolate chips on each head for eyes. Place 1 chocolate chip on each body for belly-button.

5. Bake 9 to 11 minutes or until light brown. Cool 1 minute on cookie sheet. Remove to wire racks; cool completely.

Makes 4 dozen cookies

Peanut Butter Bear

Sunflower Cookies in Flowerpots

INGREDIENTS

1 recipe Butter Cookie dough (page 82)
1 container (16 ounces) vanilla frosting
   Yellow food coloring
   Powdered sugar
1 gallon ice cream (any flavor), softened
   Chocolate decorating icing
24 chocolate sandwich cookies, crushed
1 cup shredded coconut, tinted green (see note on page 116)

SUPPLIES

12 (6-inch) lollipop sticks
6 plastic drinking straws
12 (6½-ounce) paper cups
   Pastry bag and small writing tip
12 new (3¼-inch-diameter) ceramic flowerpots, about 3½ inches tall

1. Prepare Butter Cookie Dough. Wrap in plastic wrap; refrigerate 4 hours or overnight.

2. Preheat oven to 350°F. Grease cookie sheets. Roll out dough on lightly floured surface to ⅛-inch thickness. Cut dough with 3-inch flower-shaped cookie cutter; place cut-outs on prepared cookie sheets.

3. Bake 8 to 10 minutes or until cookie edges are lightly browned. Remove to wire racks; cool completely.

4. Tint vanilla frosting desired shade of yellow with food coloring. Reserve ⅔ cup yellow frosting. Cover remaining yellow frosting; set

continued on page 116

114

Left to right: Sunflower Cookies and Daisy Cookies in Flowerpots

Sunflower Cookies in Flowerpots, continued

aside. Blend enough powdered sugar into reserved ⅔ cup yellow
frosting to make a very thick frosting. Use about 1 tablespoon
thickened frosting to attach lollipop stick to back of each cookie.
Set aside to allow frosting to dry completely.

5. Cut straws crosswise in half. Hold 1 straw upright in center of
each paper cup; pack ice cream around straw, completely filling
each cup with ice cream. (Be sure straw sticks up out of ice cream.)
Freeze 3 to 4 hours or until ice cream is hardened.

6. Frost front side of each cookie as desired with previously covered
thinner yellow frosting. Spoon chocolate icing into pastry bag fitted
with writing tip. Decorate cookies as desired.

7. To serve, clip off straw to make even with ice cream. Place ice
cream-filled cups in flowerpots. Insert lollipop stick, with cookie
attached, into opening of each straw to stand cookie upright in
flowerpot. Sprinkle ice cream with cookie crumbs to resemble dirt;
sprinkle with green coconut to resemble grass.

Makes 12 servings

Note: To tint coconut, dilute a few drops of food coloring with
½ teaspoon water in large resealable plastic food storage bag. Add
1 to 1⅓ cups flaked coconut. Seal bag; shake until coconut is evenly
colored. For a deeper color, add more diluted food coloring and
shake again.

Daisy Cookies: Cut dough into 12 circles with 1-inch cookie cutter.
Place on cookie sheet. Gather scraps of dough; shape into petals.
Arrange petals around circles to make daisies. Continue as directed
in step 3, decorating cookies as desired.

Peanut Butter Crispy Treats

6 tablespoons butter or margarine
2 (10-ounce) packages marshmallows
2 cups JIF® Creamy Peanut Butter
10 cups crisp rice cereal
   CRISCO® No-Stick Cooking Spray

GLAZE (OPTIONAL)
2½ cups sifted powdered sugar
½ cup butter or margarine
½ cup brown sugar, packed
2 tablespoons milk
1 teaspoon vanilla

In large saucepan, melt butter over low heat. Add marshmallows. Stir until completely melted and remove from heat.

Stir in JIF® and mix well to incorporate. Add cereal and stir until well coated.

Press into two 9-inch pans, well coated with CRISCO® No-Stick Cooking Spray, and allow to cool.

Combine all ingredients for glaze in a small saucepan. Cook for 2 minutes over medium heat or until sugar dissolves. Pour glaze over top of bars and allow to cool before cutting and serving.

Makes 18 servings

Note: Do not store Peanut Butter Crispy Treats in refrigerator. The moisture will cause the cereal to lose crispness. Wrap bars in plastic wrap and store in a cool and dry place.

Quick S'More

1 whole graham cracker
1 large marshmallow
1 teaspoon hot fudge sauce

1. Break graham cracker in half crosswise. Place one half on small paper plate or microwavable plate; top with marshmallow.

2. Spread remaining ½ of cracker with fudge sauce.

3. Place cracker with marshmallow in microwave. Microwave at HIGH 12 to 14 seconds or until marshmallow puffs up. Immediately place remaining cracker, fudge side down, over marshmallow. Press crackers gently to even out marshmallow layer. Cool completely.

Makes 1 serving

Tip: S'mores can be made up to 12 hours in advance and wrapped in plastic wrap or sealed in a small plastic food storage bag. Store at room temperature until ready to serve.

Twinkie® Kebobs

HOSTESS® Twinkies®, 1 for each serving
Strawberries or other fruit
Soft candies

Cut each Twinkie into four equal pieces. Stick Twinkies (through the cake, not the cream!), strawberries and soft candies on kebob rods.

Tip: For Halloween, insert your favorite Halloween candy.

Quick S'More

Dirt Bites

4½ cups party mix or crispy multigrain cereal
2 tablespoons Butter Flavor CRISCO® Shortening or Butter
Flavor CRISCO® Stick
½ cup chocolate chips
¼ cup peanut butter
½ teaspoon vanilla
¾ cup powdered sugar

Measure party mix or cereal and set aside in large mixing bowl.

Melt CRISCO® Shortening, chocolate chips and peanut butter together in saucepan on low heat (or microwave on 50% power, checking at 1 minute intervals).

Remove mixture from heat and stir in vanilla.

Pour over cereal and mix until well coated.

Add powdered sugar to zipper bag; add coated cereal and toss to coat all.

Spread double coated cereal onto sheet of wax paper to cool. Pick up coated cereal with hands and store in clean zipper bag. Discard excess sugar. Refrigerate coated cereal.   *Makes 4½ cups*

Super Suggestion!

*For individual take-home treats, wrap these
delicious Dirt Bites in festive colored cellophane.
Then tie the bundles with colored ribbon or raffia.*

Acknowledgments

The publisher would like to thank the companies and organizations listed below for the use of their recipes and photographs in this publication.

Dole Food Company, Inc.

Hershey Foods Corporation

Hostess®

Keebler® Company

© Mars, Incorporated 2004

Mott's® is a registered trademark of Mott's, Inc.

Newman's Own, Inc.®

Reckitt Benckiser Inc.

Reddi-wip® is a registered trademark of ConAgra Brands, Inc.

The J.M. Smucker Company

StarKist® Seafood Company

Texas Peanut Producers Board

Unilever Bestfoods North America

Index

METRIC CONVERSION CHART

VOLUME MEASUREMENTS (dry)

$^1/_8$ teaspoon = 0.5 mL
$^1/_4$ teaspoon = 1 mL
$^1/_2$ teaspoon = 2 mL
$^3/_4$ teaspoon = 4 mL
1 teaspoon = 5 mL
1 tablespoon = 15 mL
2 tablespoons = 30 mL
$^1/_4$ cup = 60 mL
$^1/_3$ cup = 75 mL
$^1/_2$ cup = 125 mL
$^2/_3$ cup = 150 mL
$^3/_4$ cup = 175 mL
1 cup = 250 mL
2 cups = 1 pint = 500 mL
3 cups = 750 mL
4 cups = 1 quart = 1 L

VOLUME MEASUREMENTS (fluid)

1 fluid ounce (2 tablespoons) = 30 mL
4 fluid ounces ($^1/_2$ cup) = 125 mL
8 fluid ounces (1 cup) = 250 mL
12 fluid ounces (1$^1/_2$ cups) = 375 mL
16 fluid ounces (2 cups) = 500 mL

WEIGHTS (mass)

$^1/_2$ ounce = 15 g
1 ounce = 30 g
3 ounces = 90 g
4 ounces = 120 g
8 ounces = 225 g
10 ounces = 285 g
12 ounces = 360 g
16 ounces = 1 pound = 450 g

DIMENSIONS

$^1/_{16}$ inch = 2 mm
$^1/_8$ inch = 3 mm
$^1/_4$ inch = 6 mm
$^1/_2$ inch = 1.5 cm
$^3/_4$ inch = 2 cm
1 inch = 2.5 cm

OVEN TEMPERATURES

250°F = 120°C
275°F = 140°C
300°F = 150°C
325°F = 160°C
350°F = 180°C
375°F = 190°C
400°F = 200°C
425°F = 220°C
450°F = 230°C

BAKING PAN SIZES

Utensil	Size in Inches/Quarts	Metric Volume	Size in Centimeters
Baking or Cake Pan (square or rectangular)	8×8×2	2 L	20×20×5
	9×9×2	2.5 L	23×23×5
	12×8×2	3 L	30×20×5
	13×9×2	3.5 L	33×23×5
Loaf Pan	8×4×3	1.5 L	20×10×7
	9×5×3	2 L	23×13×7
Round Layer Cake Pan	8×1½	1.2 L	20×4
	9×1½	1.5 L	23×4
Pie Plate	8×1¼	750 mL	20×3
	9×1¼	1 L	23×3
Baking Dish or Casserole	1 quart	1 L	—
	1½ quart	1.5 L	—
	2 quart	2 L	—